SCENES FROM THE LIVE POETS' SOCIETY

◆

VOL. V
2018

SCENES
FROM THE
LIVE POETS'
SOCIETY

◆

VOL. V

2018

◆

A Selection of Poems
by members of the
Live Poets' Society

FIRST EDITION 2018

10 9 8 7 6 5 4 3 2 1

LIBRARY OF CONGRESS CATALOG CARD NUMBER: 2018935370

ISBN: 978-0-938631-59-0 paper

PUBLISHED BY:

THE LIVE POETS' SOCIETY
c/o Sherry Hardage
93 Parkside Rd. SE
Rio Rancho, New Mexico 87124

INTRODUCTION

The Live Poets' Society had an interesting beginning in 1994. Richard Brandt, the founder, was inspired by the 1989 movie *The Dead Poets' Society.* It was the story of an eccentric teacher and a group of boys who meet in a secret cave to read aloud the works of "dead" poets and their own "live" creations. Richard started asking his friends, "What do you do for yourself, your guts? How do you feed your soul?" If they answered, "Write poetry," he invited them to join his new group, The Live Poets' Society.

Within two years, 20 people were meeting quarterly for lunch and readings. Now the Live Poets' Society has almost 40 members ranging in age from thirty-somethings to nonagenarians, including Brandt himself, who, at 92 years old, is still penning poems.

Brandt, a long-time resident of Santa Fe, now lives in Phoenix, Arizona. Five years ago, he turned the management of the Society over to Sherry Hardage because it was "time to hand over the reins to the next generation."

Hardage continues the tradition of meeting three to four times a year, to read poems in a space where all are welcomed and cheered, where deep friendships form and heartbreak is as common as delight.

On occasion, we Live Poets have read our work at bookstores, on the radio, and during dramatic performances. When the compulsion to share poetry overwhelms us, we publish a collection. The last book, Scenes from the *Live Poets' Society, Volume IV,* published in 2011, won the New Mexico Best Poetry Anthology.

Some of our poets are well known in the larger world of poetry for their contributions, prizes, and organizations they helped create. With this collection, our members hope to entertain and enlighten you…perhaps bring an "ah-ha moment" recognition of the emotions and situations we all experience during this passage through human existence.

THE EDITORS: *Sherry Hardage, Doris Fields, and Shari Morrison*

Live Poets' Society Membership List 2018

Olga Anson, H. Marie Aragón, Payton Auerbach, John Bishop, Meghan Carl, Glenys Carl, Peggy Marie Damiani, Victor di Suvero, Brother John Fairfax, Doris Arnette Fields, Helen Finney, Henry C. Finney, Sherry Hardage, Gerry Hotchkiss, Georgia Jones-Davis, Marilyn Kahn, Rheta Moazzami, Melanie Morais, Mary Morris, Shari Morrison, Sheila Ortego-McLaughlin, Katie Peters, Deborah Potter, Caroline Ravenfox, Robert Rhodes, Mimi Rhodes, Arden Tice, Kendra Wilson-Smith, Pamela Wolff, Michael Woodruff

Distant Out-of-Town Members

Richard Brandt, Helen Brandt, Jerry Cajko, Jessica Elkins, Bonnie Lupien, Julia Rhodes, Sally Anne Rosenberg, Marilyn Stablein

Poets who have contributed to the Live Poets' Society 5th Book of Poetry, 2018

Olga Anson, H. Marie Aragón, Richard Brandt, Victor di Suvero, Jessica Elkins, Doris Arnette Fields, Sherry Hardage, Georgia Jones-Davis, Rheta Moazzami, Shari Morrison, Sheila Ortego-McLaughlin, Robert Rhodes, Mimi Rhodes, Sally Anne Rosenberg, Michael Woodruff,

and Judge Wyatt Heard (in memoriam)

Poets Contributing to this volume

Olga Anson

Olga Anson's creative spirit began as a child as she day-dreamed on the adobe porches and in the apple orchards of her grandparents in Northern New Mexico. She is a native of the Land of Enchantment and a graduate of the University of New Mexico. Her career in social services and educational guidance took her to live in California, Nevada, and Colorado. Travel to New Zealand, France, and Germany further inspired her awe for the natural world and fueled her desire to express the deeply personal feelings universally shared in human experience. As a singer-songwriter, she combines her music with many of the poems. Her topics range from a love for Mother Earth's ecology to transformative life experiences.

KATRINA LEVEL 5

They say a hurricane's comin',
We've got to evacuate the city
Pack up all our belongin's,
Katrina — they say she's a level 5

Her landfall leveled the Gulf Coast
Wiped out Mobile, Gulfport and New Orleans
Levees they been busted, water 15 foot and risin'
Worst natural disaster the U.S. has ever seen

Roads and bridges wiped out, debris and destruction everywhere
Houses left lookin' like match sticks
Scale of human suffering like we've nev ah seen before
No way to stop the fury of over hundred twenty mile winds

Katrina levelled the Gulf Coast, August 2000 and 5
The poor, the sick, the feeble, left behind to die

"Help us, Help us", we're screaming at the cameras
Bring us fresh water, and supplies
We're waitin' at the Superdome bus stop
Praying Lord that we don't die

I tried hard to hold her but the wat uh wouldn't let me
I tried but she still slipped away
"Poppa, take care of our chill'un"
Last words I heard her say.

continues ➹

I'm walkin' in this water, with bodies floatin' by
They say it's just a toxic stew
I put my faith in the man who walked on water
Prayin' Lord you'll see me through

A lifetime of toil now just rubble, but it won't destroy our dreams
We'll come back to build our cit y, the grand ol' cit y of New Orleans
The birthplace of jazz, Louis Armstrong, ol' Satchmo
Pete Fountain and all that jaaaazzzzz

Our hearts may be broken,
But our spirts will rise again

Lord, we're a righteous people
And we will endure
We're still alive, fightin' to survive
Our hearts may be broken, but our spirits will rise again
Our spirits will riiise again, O yeah, O yeaah

LAND OF ENCHANTMENT

Land of Enchantment, "O fair New Mexico"
Zia sun, symbol of life's circle
Four seasons, four directions
Four times of day, four stages of human life

Zia symbol binding ancient mystery and people in harmony.
Archeological treasure chest—ancient sea beds, fossils, hidden cities and kivas.
Taos Pueblo, sacred *adobe,* hearth and home
continuously occupied for over a thousand years.
Native American spiritual ties reveal the origins of Mother Earth and her people.
A history over 400 years old of hardy Spanish colonists and their descendants.
Sixteenth century Spanish colloquialisms
endure in the high mountain villages *Del Norte.*
Anglos with artistic sensibilities
craving wide open spaces and freedom from convention.
The Manhattan project, the Trinity site, developed the A bomb
Genesis of atomic age new technology.

Land of *Milagro*—home of *Penitente* and prayer
Santuario de Chimayo—pilgrimage site
Canes, braces, crutches cast off
Testimonials on walls
Sight restored to the blind,
The lame made to walk,
 "*Tierra bendita*" cures all ailments.
Santa Fe's miraculous stairway to heaven at the Loretto chapel.
San Francisco de Asis, the most painted and photographed church in the world,
Taos harbor for "Shadow of the Cross",
a mysterious painting with the cross that only becomes
visible when it glows in the dark
while Jesus walks on water.
Santa Fe opera—music of angels in an outdoor amphitheater under crisp desert sky

continues ➚

Scenic wonders — *Sangre de Cristo* Mountains,
Valles Caldera largest caldera in the US next to Yellowstone
Ojo Caliente, healing geothermal mineral waters,
White sand dunes of pure gypsum crystals
perfect emergency landing strip for Roswell's 1947 UFO alien sightings.

Familia, horno and home branded into the soul.
Rarified air in *Sandia* colored mountains works up the appetite for
Calabacitas, posole eaten for goodluck on New Year's Eve,
Tamales wrapped in maize husks, multi-colored Indian corn kernels.
The original Hatch *chile* green burrito, no veggie wrap masquerade,
Red or green, you know what I mean,
Yet, somehow it's always Christmas.

Luminaria bonfires and *farolitos* guide the way home.
"Volver, Volver" Mariachi song of heartache calls out in the night,
"O Fair New Mexico"
Land of Enchantment.

O, CARELESS LOVE

Not a day goes by that I don't miss you
Not a day passes without a tear
Could I have held you any closer?
I told you of my love, daily, yet today it does not seem enough.
If I could have but one more day with you, it still would not be enough.
I wish I'd never gone away
I thought the roses would always be in bloom
Their fragrance was an opiate. It took me to another world
Where there was no death, nor sadness, and,
An elixir of immortality would keep us forever young.
I did not see the wrinkles, nor the color fading from your hair
Or if I did, I do not remember, so tightly I pressed you to my breast.
Old age, it crept up so slowly, I did not hear the knell.
You were snatched away from me so cruelly
As if by some surreptitious vampire in the night
Now I find myself without you,
How quickly did I fall from heaven into hell.

You are in another realm of existence, one of which I know little,
Small glimpses I'm allowed to sporadically see
Occasional visits in dreams,
Your possessions packed in boxes
Left behind, small treasures—photographs and memory.
Where is that balm in Gilead that heals the heart-sick soul?

SOLAR RAYCE SONG 2003

The American Solar Challenge
Chicago to L.A.
Two thousand miles of solar raycing
America USA

Hi-tech solar cells and
Cars that look like spaceships
It's a solar rayce
Rollin' down old route sixty six

Battery's good, Sun is high
Turn it on now and let me fly
Solar kicks
Rollin' down ole route 66

Start stage two, at Rolla,
Tulsa, Miami, Oklahoma
No more rain; it's a five-mile gain
Lord, don't let me take the wrong turn now

Rollin' wheels, Fast food meals
Amarillo's only half way
Take me on down to Start Stage Three
Here I come Albuquerque

Flagstaff, Kingman, Winslow, Arizona
Start Stage 4 at Barstow, California
Hot and cramped, help me make it please
What I wouldn't give now for 75 degrees and just a slight breeze
Dreamin' of the lights of L.A.

Battery's good, Sun is high
Turn it on now and let me fly
Solar kicks
Rollin' down ole route sixty-six

The idea for the poem/song germinated at the 2003 Taos Solar Music Festival where Dick and Olga Anson met with New Mexico Solar Energy Association to plan the July 17-20, 2003 American Solar Challenge Stage Three Expo stopover at The University of New Mexico Pit.

Written to publicize the event, encourage the solar car teams and cheer them on to victory, words express the driver's point of view focused on crossing a distant two-thousand mile finish line in a Solar Car Rayce from Chicago to Los Angeles on The Historic Mother Road, Route 66.

Qualification for the event made each participant a winner on the cutting edge of a new technology with memories of a lifetime. A special thank you to Dick Anson who provided technical knowledge and helped bring the project to fruition.

WEST COAST HUSTLE

Vacation is a thousand miles away
Driving on a gray ribbon of highway

I can smell the salt air of the ocean
And feel the beach sand in my toes
The cold Pacific water on my bare feet
Fuchsia red sunsets and endless horizons

Bicycle on a path off the San Luis Rey river
Down to the mission, timing is crucial
It's a cold head wind on a Western track
If we're too late on our way back

Walks on the West Coast's longest wooden pier
Delight us with dolphins jumping parallel to the coast.

I walk hand in hand with you wading in water
An electric plant in the distance,
Who else holds the Guinness world record for that walk?
Your take on life is magical

Surfers at Swami's Meditation Gardens
bless us with lotus blossoms and koi.

Bully II an English Pub's calamari strips in Carmel
And our search for the perfect calamari is on.
Fresh seafood on the Barbie, hot tub soaks
We laugh like there's no tomorrow.

Vay-K ends before it begins
The vibration of the road, strange no-tell hotel beds.
It feels like a month of Sundays.
The desert never ends
Joshua trees, Ocotillo, Saguaro, Cane cactus.
Are we there yet?

Finally, we turn onto Our Street
There's no place like home.

H. Marie Aragón

H. Marie Aragón lives and writes in view of the Ortiz and Cerrillos Mountains, dry arroyos and the grass lands of Eldorado at Santa Fe, New Mexico. Here she found gold — a sanctuary in the writing community of the High Desert Poets. In this section her varied styles evoke a sense of intimacy, vulnerability and presence of young men as they experience the events of war.

H. Marie Aragon's poetry has been published in various journals and anthologies. In 2014 her work was featured in a mini feature in Malpaís Review. She won the 2015 LUMMOX Prize for Poetry which resulted in a chapbook titled, *When Desert Willows Speak.* Presently Marie is working on a manuscript of poems for publication.

RIDING THE OLD SANTA FE SOUTHERN
Philip Z. Aragón 1947 – 1995

1.

Camp Pendleton   January 1968.
"Can you take orders?" barks the drillmaster.
"Sir   yes   Sir!"
"How do you know you can take orders?"
"Sir   I have five older sisters   sir."

2.

In a photo you guard
a Viet Cong prisoner—
hands tied behind his back,
gunnysack over his head.
Your hand rests on his shoulder.
You hold a large jungle-leaf
to shade his sweaty body—
a simple gesture in a sweltering war zone.
Sleepless nights, wooden rosary beads worn,
St. Christopher medal pinned in your uniform pocket.

3.

After Nam you walk into mass
at Mount St. Francis Chapel.
Nuns stand to sing
"Onward Christian Soldiers."

4.

My first night alone in Santa Fe—
empty house, vast sky, dark storm clouds.
I call the real estate agent.
"Put my house back on the market!"
She brings Mikey, an old Border-collie mix
to keep me company. I needed protection!

continues ➚

5.

That night in a dream you visit me
riding the Old Santa Fe Southern.
You sit calmly wearing a fedora.
"I'll be your protector—no need for a dog,
and you won't have to feed me," you laugh.
I settle into my new home.

6.

Today Memorial Day I place your photo
and a small United States Marine Corp flag
next to a vase of wild iris.
I light a votive candle
to honor your valor, courage, and love.
Philip my brother, I salute you.

Philip Zoilo Aragón served as a corporal in
the United States Marines Corp
in Viet Nam 1968–1969.

OFRENDA FOR PHILIP

Marine Corp photo —
young   innocent,
your cross   Viet Nam heavy.

I arrange your ofrenda
on a smoky-blue *colcha* shawl,
votive candles to light your way.

Agua Santa para saciar tu sed.
Peaches, plums — sweet nectar
for your night passage.

Sunflower seeds and *una cerveza fría.*
Chocolate *calavera* —
P h i l i p written across its forehead.

Orange Marigold petals
soften your barefoot journey.
What more can I offer?

Silent for twenty years —
no way to escape.
Agent Orange ambushes your lungs.

Bells ring a mournful tone,
a single trumpet, a folded flag.
Winged horses carry you home.

*Hoy, Día de los Muertos
estás presente como en los
años antes de tu muerte.

*Today, *Dia de los Muertos*
you are present as in the
years before your death.

Published in *When Desert Willows Speak,* 2015 by H. Marie Aragón

MY BROTHER THE GHOST

"Is it true that all life comes from the mountain?" Taos Pueblo Chief Biano asked.
"Yes, where there is water there is life," Jung replied.

Life for my brother began in a farm house
near a stream of muddy water
shaded by tall cottonwoods
near fields of sweet corn
in the distance—a tall mountain range.

He painted his tricycle red.
He painted his bicycle white.
He painted his car blue.

My brother went to Viet Nam,
returned with a hungry ghost in his lungs.
He married
had a son, had a daughter
went to college
worked for the city.
Twenty years later the ghost appeared
calling out it's name—
Agent Orange.

In an old mission church in *San Luis*
El Día de Los Muertos procession begins.
We sing old Spanish songs.
Smoke from palm ashes fills the air
candy *calaveras* line in the vestibule
votive candles flicker on the altar
petals of marigold cover the aisle—
guiding the spirits return.

Father Benevides reads each name of the deceased,—PHILIP!
In unison the congregation shouts—*P R E S E N T E !*
I fall to my knees.

On the last rib of *Los Cristos,*
along the river bed
where all life begins,
my brother's spirit returns
each year for a ghostly dance

CHIEF JOSEPH MEDICINE CROW
1913 – 2016

The boy, "High Bird"
taught in the tradition of warrior by his father —
tracking, hand to hand combat,
endurance and honor
was prepared for WWII.   '

Far from his Montana reservation
deep behind enemy lines
in snow-covered hills of France,
High Bird tracked horses with his field glasses
to a farmyard beyond the river.

He waited until dawn colored the horizon in shades of fire —
orange, magenta, violet, replaced night shadows.

High Bird advanced on foot —
three red war-stripes painted on his body,
under his camouflage jacket.
A sacred eagle feather tucked in his helmet —
protection medicine given by his father.

He neared the camp in combat boots,
though his steps were as light as deer-skin moccasins.
Fifty thoroughbreds corralled in the barnyard
stood watchful yet calm under his spell.

High Bird tied a bridle out of a piece of rope,
mounted a sorrel with the braided mane
and raced from the camp screaming a Crow war cry.

Horses stampeded at full gallop
snorting as they raced behind the lead mare.
In the barn, German SS officers awaken.
Wearing only underwear, they fired their Lugers.

Safe beyond the distant hills,
High Bird softly sang a Crow honor song.

Chief Joseph Medicine Crow, last war chief of the plains Indian Crow Nation, was raised on the Crow reservation in Montana. He earned a graduate degree in anthropology from University of California. Joseph Medicine Crow, "High Bird", received an honorary doctoral degree for his work as a historian of the Crow Nation.

During WWII Joseph Medicine Crow served in the 103 Infantry Division. During that time he completed four essential "tasks" that earned him the title of Chief, one of which was to steal an enemy's horse. Chief Medicine Crow was a recipient of the Presidential Medal of Freedom and the French Legion of Honor for his service during the war. He died in April 2016.

KNIGHT OF THE DIVINE WIND
MITSUO OSAKI 1929 – 2017

1.

He didn't tell father
until he walked into the garden
wearing the uniform of a *Kamikaze* pilot.
Mitsuo, third son was seventeen.
His father threw down his watermelon,
silent before he spoke —
"Come home my son. Don't die!"

2.

Under the *Bushido* code —
loyalty and honor until death
Mitsuo trained for his mission.
He wrote a final letter home,
perhaps a death poem.
In a farewell ceremony
he drank sake from a porcelain cup —
a gift from the emperor.

3.

He boarded a *Mitsubishi* Zero
wearing a *senninbari,*
the belt of one-thousand stitches —
a gift from his mother.
He tied on the Rising Sun headband.

In the wake of death
three times his fate was sealed —
    June — engine failure
      July — runway bombed
        August — Emperor Hirohito surrendered.

4.

In his garden beneath a persimmon tree
Mitsuo sipped macha tea
with spirits of brothers remembered.
At eighty-eight — his final flight
Mitsuo was carried home
on wings of a single white crane.

A BOY'S UNCERTAIN JOURNEY

On the nightly news, a Syrian boy
walks along the railroad, his clothes
tied in a bed sheet thrown over his shoulder.

Behind him the dim light of a crescent moon—
Lamp of Heaven and Earth fades as ISIS fells
The Temple of Bel—Bride of the Desert.

Ahead of him Hungarian soldiers
guard the border with razor-wire fences,
rubber bullets, and tear gas grenades.

Ahead of him tired and hungry refugees pack
into Keleti Train Station and sleep on cardboard beds
as they wait for German-bound trains.

The boy doesn't know his birthplace
is being erased from maps,
replaced by names in unfamiliar languages.
He knows only of hunger and thirst.
Pita, hummus, olives and cheese linger.
Shoes once comfortable are now tight.
His feet are blistered and sore.
For a moment he sets down his heavy bundle.

He whistles and waits as his pigeons fill the sky —
wings out-stretched, free to cross borders,
to feed on ripe grain, and to sleep in feathered nests.

Richard Brandt

BIOGRAPHY
requires
GEOGRAPHY
And in this case—
LEXICOGRAPHY

Born: YES
Location of Birth: PLANET EARTH
Location now: PLANET EARTH
Having spent most of my life between
mathematics and the entertainment industry,
why did I invent the Live Poets' Society?

Answer:
IT'S EXCITING!
POET MEMBERS ARE FASCINATING!!
WE ARE ALL A BIT CRAZY!!!
It's wonderful to write and read poetry—
even at the age of 90 !!!!!!!

IN THE BEGINNING

Were I a God Olympian
With unbound awesome powers
To create exotic life on lonely distant planets

Were I a God Olympian
How should I make decisions
What species would I place on some newborn world

Were I a God Olympian
I'd need to study carefully
Considering possibilities; mountains, caverns, lakes

Were I a God Olympian
I'd first converse with Zeus
Who better to translate for me our universe untamed

Were I a God Olympian
I'd want an audience with Hera
To understand the female psyche and the birthing process

Were I a God Olympian
I'd approach fair Aphrodite
To hear vast notions of love, beauty, and the sea

Were I a God Olympian
I'd seek revered Apollo
In the evening, lyre in hand, chariot quietly at rest

Were I a God Olympian
I'd listen quietly to Athena
That keen and brilliant mind that clearly conquers all

There were Goddesses and Gods surrounding me
    On Olympus, my decision came to be
        Based on mythical advice about tomorrow

continues ➶

I'd start with merely footprints in the sand
    Nearby an ocean tide two figures stand
        Adding memories of joys and sometimes sorrows

    Yes, both families and structures they would build
    Would this become the purpose and their goals
    Yet like puppets on my string and unfulfilled
    Afraid, they'd pray for me to save their souls

    Or should I invent a fascinating garden
    Including twisting snakes and fruitful trees
    Let's start with Paradise, a man and woman
    Such perfection, no more fears nor enemies

    Conceptually conjectural
    And somewhat ineffectual
    Yet with powers intellectual
    And surely highly sexual
    With abilities perpetual
    Including architectural

Were I a God Olympian
I'd continue rearranging
Creating different worlds, experimenting, changing

Were I a God Olympian
I believe that my mistakes
Would sadly leave each planet a mass of crumbling quakes

Were I a God Olympian
My final thought would be
Please let Eden live and never bother me

TRY TO REMEMBER
(The 60s)

Imagine, for a moment, a gathering of a generation
The sad, the hopeful, the flower children—and I am there
It's the 60s, we're singing together—in harmony
Bob Dylan in one corner, Paul Simon over there

And the women, Mary Travers, and Janis Ian—it's a love-in
Even Eleanor Rigby and Mrs. Robinson walk right in
Behind her Billy Joe—he's alive and well—and Georgy Girl
Where is this magical place and time of peace and understanding?

Imagine, for a moment, it's a party at Alice's Restaurant
The Vietnam war rages—Pete Seeger arrives
Even that Girl from Ipanema, looking straight ahead, not at me
It's a passion, it's a protest, the Utopia of tomorrow

I arrive slightly depressed—I think I'm goin' out of my head
The conversation dangles, strange ideas blowin' in the wind
Where have all the flowers gone
Raindrops keep falling on my head

Imagine, for a moment, only the sound of silence is heard
Then Pete says, "turn, turn, turn"
Alan and Marilyn remind us, "it's in the windmills of your mind"
Bob claims, "the times they are a'changin"

Suddenly, Rado and Ragni exclaim
       "The Moon is in the Seventh House"
Then Pete asserts strongly
       "For Every Thing There Is A Season"
Arlo shouts
       "You Can Get Anything You Want"
But Melina says quietly
       "Never On Sunday"

We had roamed newly liberated with Kerouac on the road
We came from San Francisco with flowers in our hair
We all now move together like a rolling stone
We touch, we groan—I become gentle on my mind

Imagine, for the moment, this beat generation has us convinced

  It's The Time of Aquarius!
      We Shall Overcome!
         Up, Up, and Away

BLUES AND THE RAINBOW
(VIBGYOR)

Some color shades remind us we're in trouble
A blackened hole some day might burst our bubble
So many tints express our secret worries
Our blue sky blocked at ties by whitened flurries

> Reflect a moment please:

>> How red brings up the threat of nearby danger
>> How green infects us with jealous envy
>> How yellow corresponds to fear and illness
>> How grey conveys the signal of our aging
>> ---------and, of course, there is the blue of painful sadness

Yet colors of the rainbow pierce our gloom
Predicting pleasant things will grow and bloom
Shout VIBGYOR in chorus all as one
And blow away the clouds that hide our sun

> V for Violet—proves that flowers bloom in Spring
> I for Indigo—gleams a plant in all its beauty
> B for Blue—informs us truly there's a heaven
> G for Green—means our fields are surely sprouting
> Y for Yellow—glows romantic in the moonlight
> O for Orange—tastes for us the sweetest marmalade
> R for Red—shows our blood is warmly flowing

Thus when each of us might feel we have the blues
Remember how to make it all good news

> Shout:

(All together now) VIBGYOR!!!

ETERNITY
(In both directions)

How many stars in heaven
How many heavens in our universe
How many universes exist in our time
Is time a wormhole to our past and future

We can move around, up, down and sideways
To any of the three dimensions
Length, width and height is where we reside in space
Yet time is our fourth dimension
        Can we travel backwards or sideways in time
        Are we limited to moving forward minute by minute
        Is each minute always sixty seconds

Yet Einstein informs us time is a fourth dimension
All four dimensions are warped by gravity
If we travel near the speed of light, we age much slower
When that lady astronaut spends several years in space
        At enormous speeds and returns to Earth
        Her husband awaiting her landing is now ancient
        Having aged much more than she

Confusion therefore is unlimited in our minds
What is the reality of ever expanding infinity
Combined with the possibility of ongoing eternity
Perhaps no ends exist in space nor time
        Universes have multiplied, time is forever
        Humanity may some day crawl into that wormhole
        Allowing us to visit our distant past and future

Victor di Suvero

Victor began writing when he was 16. The continuing interest Victor has had in poetry's return to a central place in society, has manifested itself in the work he has done with the establishment of PEN New Mexico. He was a member of the board of the National Poetry Association in San Francisco for five years and served as events coordinator for National Poetry Week in 1988 which has since evolved into National Poetry Month in April of each year sponsored by the Poetry Society of America and a group of major Publishers and University Presses across the country. He was a founding director of the New Mexico Book Association and a central figure in the presentation of New Mexico at the International Book Fair in Guadalajara, Mexico in 1994. He is also responsible for the publication of *¡Saludos! Poemas de Nuevo Mexico,* the first bilingual anthology of the poetry of New Mexico. He has published 14 books of poems in his lifetime and has been featured in dozens of anthologies. Once nominated Poet Laureate of Santa Fe, he was appointed Poet Laureate of Brookedale Senior Living, where he now resides.

THE BUSINESS OF POETRY

The business of poetry
>is more than the arrangement of readings, the
trading of favors, the wooing of audiences, or
the management of notices, of schedules and
publications.

The business of poetry
>is more than the evocation of feelings, the
confrontation of falsehoods, the creation of
visions of order and the promise of bountiful
pleasures.

The business of poetry
>is more than a transaction for dinner, or
solace, or recognition or even of vengeance.

The business of poetry
>is more than an advertisement for love
discovered, uncovered, appreciated or lost.

The business of poetry
>is the recognition of that which is true, which
brings us face to face with ourselves in the
morning and with laughter at noon.

The business of poetry
>is the flight of the kestrel, the throat of the
jaguar and the sound of a frozen river
breaking to run in the spring.

It is the recognition of the child by the father
>and the song of the mother at evening.

It is that which makes the heart glad, the
>harvest bountiful and permits hope to
rise up once more in the throat of the weary.

The business of poetry is poetry.

WAKING

Waking this morning in my own bed
Wondering if the trip taken was a month
Or an eternity ago.
                            Was it dream or
An illusion generated by an appetite
To discover pieces of my past and of
My future, consulting relatives in
Rome and Venice, the oracle at Delphi
The stones of Troy and the merchants
In Istanbul
I wake amazed
That I am here at all knowing
The voyage was as tangible as
The color blue in the Blue Mosque
Overlooking the Golden Horn with
Each tile more blue than sea
Or sky have ever been.
                            How can I now
Manage to put all the tales
Of my Histories together
To make a mosaic
Meaningful to others?
                            Diligence,
Determination and Dame Fortune are all
Called upon to help and yet when I call
There is no one here except myself
Waking from a dream, to a life that is
The life that I am living.

TIME IS ALL WE HAVE

It is really all we have, to give, to use, to
Share with the beloved. Time is all we have
Given to us as long as body's strength
Permits us life — all else does not belong
To us — stewards of one kind or another,
Caretakers or wastrels, good ones,
Bad ones and some in between, solitary,
Gregarious, committeed to a cause or to
Acquisitions, we share this passage we call time
While doing all the other things we do.

We sleep, sing, dance and work, bring
Children into the world while undoing
Enemies as well as animals and birds.
With each and every act of ours we use
Pieces of our capital without remorse.
Every single thing takes time — sleep
Takes time, stupidity as well — as the one
Argument for the good life is economy
Achieved by not wasting time on guilt,
Regrets or even penances.

                                Time's faces, the dark
One and the light, are the faces of our
Lives — sad and somber, serious and
Wondrous, bright and full of laughter,
From one moment to another when we
Notice their reflections
In our lives.

TRAIN OF LIFE

It's like being on the train of life
With a ticket from here to there
And she got on when I was fifty six
And got off when I had just turned ninety
The countryside was beautiful
For most of the way and we did
Manage some very difficult delays
And continued to hang on.
                              Amazing,
There were no really hard surprises
And when we crossed some difficulties
Always managed to hang on and yet
The wonder of the canyons, the deserts
And the prairies that we crossed
Kept pleasing both of us with
Positive surprises and delights.

Yes, the train of life goes into countrysides
That are boring from time to time
But the underlying murmur of the wheels
On the train tracks gives a steadiness
Equivalent to the beating of the heart
When all is well and it is morning.

YES, I HAVE SAID THIS BEFORE

Yes, as I have said before
I have come to this place in my life
Where I am tired of playing a part
In the theater of my ancestors
All these years I have had to be
A descendant of my mother's family line
That dates back to the time
Of the First Crusade as well as
My father's line dating back some
Five hundred years as bankers
In and around Venice in Italy
Good for me to have learned
All these important stories so that
I can now summarize them,
And pass them on so as to never have
To deal with them again.

All that is the business of "Then"
And all I am interested in
Is the business of "Now"
Where the sun sets and rises
One day at a time.

RITUAL

I do my exercise class in the morning
In order to stay in shape. The moves
Are the same every day and demand
Full attention reminding me when
I was an altar boy supporting every
Move the priest made during mass.
Repetition as a function of ritual.
Belief systems established times ago
Established how we repeat gestures
In order to maintain validity
As mass at the Vatican in Rome
Does not differ from one solemnized
In a shanty town church in the heart
Of Africa or the dark churches
In the Far East.
                        How we move
And when we move will maintain
The system and become as established
As the evening prayers said at
The setting of the sun over which
We have no control.
                        It is the ritual
That will maintain the belief system
We all live by anywhere
On this earth we call home.

Jessica Elkins

Jessica Lyn Elkins grew up in a small town in the Texas Panhandle. She moved to New Mexico in 1968 where she lived for 44 years. She earned a BA from the University of New Mexico and graduated from St. John's College of Santa Fe with an MA in Liberal Education. A varied career path included stints as a general contractor, ice cream shop owner, and human resources manager for automobile dealerships. She had previously submitted to *Scenes from the Live Poets Society* in 2001 and 2003. These current poems reflect inspiration found in her new home in North Central Florida. Jessica Elkins has published two books, *The Friend in Question* (2015), a novel about friendship, coincidences, and betrayal between two friends and *A Coyote Taught Me Poetry: Poetry and Prose Reflections from The Land of Enchantment to the Sunshine State* (2016).

A WALK IN THE WOODS

Sun shower ceases and dripping leaves tremble
by the soft path illuminated with wet silver drops.

Pale light falls on dusky green stumps run over
by trailing ferns shaken by moist air.

Bending leafy hands to forest floor in homage to the carpet of rotted leaves
tiny sprouts of laurels sway with shining drops of rain.

An undercurrent of humming insects fill branches overhead
small sounds from birds that watch the walker from hidden perches.

Moldering pile of bricks rooted to the ground
left by careless builder as altar to the forgotten forest.

Dainty white flowers mass along the path in rectangle of sunshine
yellow centers blinking like drowsy eyes of a child.

Surrounded in the slowly stirring canopy of towering oaks and pines
An awakened heart find wonder and peace.

CRY OF THE MOTHER

Harsh cry comes from mother
hidden in the high branch of ancient oak.
Urgent, pleading, demanding obedience
to learn the wild independence of being hawk.

Somewhere close by young bird quivers with fear
of standing alone without the mother's presence
the only safety known in her sheltered life.

Mother hawk calls again again again
instinctive, wild, urging a summer's nest single progeny to fly,
rise on dusky wings, feel what a hawk should feel
glide into the trees and silently land by insistent parent.

Learn the lesson and become what she will be—
predator, cloud flyer, reigning royalty
of miles of earth and sky.

MORNING: ON THE PORCH

Stillness of air
Rustling in trees
Birds unseen in woods

A rush of wings
Two wrens tumbling through
The early golden light

Breathing soft green pasture grass
Leaves of tall oaks
Bright flowers ready for
Bees and butterflies to awake.

Waiting, Watching, Waiting
Watching, Waiting, Watching
For time to begin.

AT SUNSET: ON THE PORCH AGAIN

Glowing from the west
    forest floor of fiery red leaves

A carpet of shining
    silent oaks rooted in shimmer of gold

Long shadows
    flame red patches among wistful gray clouds

Sun sinking behind tall guardians
    dark green cedars cling to back-lit black

Who am I to question life's answers?

WHAT I NEED TODAY

Lord, I need a double rainbow today.

A hummingbird in the garden might help, too.
A flight of egrets outlined dark against the eastern sky,
Maybe even a mockingbird singing with all his heart and soul in the oak tree.
It would be nice to see a sun shower glinting in the morning sun, soft sounds to
        mimic my own tears.
Another comfort would be two dogs at my side with adoring brown eyes,
        loving and loyal at my side.

And while I sat in my self-pity, helpless in my stew of thoughts
You sent all these signs.
Reminders that there is good in our world—the faithful who love—the promise of dawn—
the bird that sings a melody for another day.

With all the signs You sent, Lord, I'll plug the holes in my heart—
        gaping spaces of uncertainty and loss.

FIVE SISTER OAKS

Whisper to me
Tell me of the days
Time long past, slow, sprouting growth
Five acorns buried and forgotten
Five saplings, rain thirsty, breeze blown, sun warmed
You nodded to each other.

Whisper to me
Tell me of the years
Drought, fires, storms
Never took your secluded home
Creatures ran by, used your shade, ate your hardy acorns
You reached for each other.

Whisper to me
Tell me of the decades
Men marched, farmers cleared,
Fences wrapped between your trunks
Other trees came grew in your space
You grew close, embraced each other.

Whisper to me of the century
Histories past, stories told, wars raged
Millions died, millions born, new hopes bloomed
Five trunks reaching upward to southern light
Heavy limbs touched the earth and rooted again
You grew stronger and aged together.

Whisper to me
Tell me of the days, years, decades and century
What your enjoined trunks and limbs have given
Enriching, nourishing this one place
Five silent living witnesses
Five living sister oaks.

APRIL DAY'S DEMISE

When she was old my mother always asked
Where does the day go?

The weeks and the months
speed toward the last day
pulsing steadily, oblivious to heart beat
that will someday slow and stop.

When did time accelerate
or am I accelerating
able to open, blink, and then shut
my dazzled eyes for sleep?

The smell of wet grass
dog dozing on pine porch floor
shocking red cardinal lands on low branch of maple tree
devout squirrel with praying paws sitting meditation

Twenty-four hours from now
I will be sitting here again.
How did the April day pass?
Where did the day go?

COREOPSIS ECSTASY

If I parked my car on the roadside shoulder to examine a glorious mass of yellow coreopsis
would someone speeding by wonder why I pulled over?

If I was out of my car standing in the middle of the patch of quivering golden flowers
would someone in short tight pants bicycling past wonder why I was laughing?

If I was taking a photo of mysterious dark flower eyes in the middle of radiating disks
of vivid light would someone slow a roaring motorcycle and think how odd that someone
would stand in tall weeds so close to nodding flower faces?

If I sat in a lotus position or knelt on my knees with brilliant flower suns tickling my arms
and legs would someone in an old blue Honda wonder if I was praying to an unknown nature
god in the middle of the day?

If I was flat on my back with golden sunshine petals just inches above my nose and arms
outstretched in sweet wild surrender and singing 'Alleluia, Alleluia'
would someone in a red truck dial 911 to report a woman lying in wildflowers
at mile marker thirty one?

Doris Fields

Dr. Doris Fields is a spiritual scholar, working to foster uplift of our people (all people), as much as possible. She is also a poet, writing workshop facilitator, visual artist, retired public health worker, and retired adjunct faculty at the University of New Mexico. At her core, Fields is a spiritual seeker of understanding, wisdom, and justice; in fact her life's work is social justice. Her basic spiritual practice is compassion and humility, and these are expressed in her poetry often. Sometimes she is successful in the practice, but remembers that practice is the goal. Fields has written two books of poetry, *Hambone, Hambone, Have You Heard and Smellin' M'Self,* and has read her work nationally and internationally. Her poetry has appeared in all five volumes of *Scenes from the Live Poets' Society.* It is hoped that the reader may find evidence of her quest for understanding, wisdom, and justice in the poems included in this volume. Certainly, for her, poetry is a survival tool.

IN REMEMBRANCE

We must never forget   May their memories be a blessing

Sweet and innocent children of our world
Voter registrars: James Earl Chaney, Andrew Goodman, and Michael Schwerner
50 years ahead of us
Young school boys in Israel: Eyal Yifrach, Gilad Shaar and Naftali Fraenkel
Young school boy in the outskirts of Jerusalem: Mohammed Abu Kheidr
Nearly 300 young school girls in Nigeria whose names we do not know
Sad commentary on how we treat girls disparately even in tragedy
—we do not even know their names
Still, we must never forget

We must speak out for one another
Even if not a Jewish school boy nor a Jew at all
Even if not a Palestinian boy nor a Palestinian at all
Even if not a Nigerian school girl nor Black person at all
You do not have to be me to support my struggle
In resistance, we must speak out for one another
Lest the fundamentalists take us down one by one
Lest the extremists eat a hole into our souls one child at a time
Lest the moderates stand by and watch
As our freedom to learn, pray, and think dissolve inch by inch
Our silence will not protect us
It never has   it never will

The nearly 300 young Nigerian girls are not married off -PERIOD
They are sold into slavery
Forced so-called marriage is slavery, and is not unusual
It is not limited to Nigeria
It is wide-spread
Check out Uganda
How about Rwanda
Bolivia
Somalia
Peru
Burundi
Cambodia
And other places

continues ↗

Extremism must be confronted head on
Extremists are continuing to destroy our children

Wholesale subscription to fundamentalism or misogyny is murder
We must translate the terms
"wedding" and "bride" to their true meanings: rape and torture
Just as we taste our tears of bitterness
Also, we must remember the sweetness of their smiles

As we feel their loss permeate our bodies
Also, we must remember the joy each brought to their families

As for all our children
Only cowards would kidnap a child
The lowest form of humankind would rape a child
My child
Your child Everyone's child
Should know freedom
Every child deserves to be enveloped in love
Our arms holding them in safety
It is not new, the killing of young people like you
James Earl Chaney, Andrew Goodman, and Michael Schwerner
Eyal Yifrach, Gilad Shaar and Naftali Fraenkel
Mohammed Abu Kheidr
Nearly 300 young Nigerian school girls whose names we do not know

We remember the children of Sarajevo
of San Salvador
of West Bank
of Afghanistan
of Ireland
of Tibet
of Detroit
of Gaza
of Katrina
of Dachau
of Money, Mississippi
of Sudan
of Zulus
of Xhosas
of Birmingham
of Uganda
of Bergen-Belsen
of Crow Creek

continues ⤴

of Auschwitz
of Treblinka
of Tiguex
of Zia
of Sobibor
of the Hutus
of the Tutsis

Three young voter registrars in Mississippi
Three young school boys in Israel
One young boy in Jerusalem
And nearly 300 young school girls in Nigeria whose names we do not know
Sweet children of innocence
Absorbing all light
You are homeless
Or you are dead
Tonight

Your memories rest in the cradle of our hearts
We whisper your names from our lips
We rise to your resilience
We rise to you

I ask that we rise for a moment of silence
In respect and honor of all the lost children

Victims of genocide   terrorism   fanaticism   fear
Hatred anti-Semitism   misogyny   racism

 (SILENCE)

May our memories of them bless us

July 2014

I was deeply honored to be asked by distinguished members of the Jewish Federation of New Mexico to write a poem to read during a vigil in honor of the three Jewish boys and nearly 300 Nigerian girls who had been kidnapped. By the date of the vigil, all three Jewish boys had been killed, a young Palestinian boy had been killed, and the Nigerian girls had and have not been found.* In this poem, I attempt to call us all to bring our best selves forward, to practice compassion and understanding, and to respect all.

* On Wednesday, May 18, 2016, one of the abducted Nigerian girls, Amina Ali Darsha Nkeki, was discovered along with a baby girl on the outskirts of the Sambisa forest.

SILENCING EYES DIVERTING CULTURE

I looked like misery to you   my face the only mirror I had to offer
still you saw misery always did
long before your darker eyes   met my dark cheeks
before you had reality   to attach to your experience with me

I spoke to you through black lips thick as Tennessee
you looked through me with Oklahoma eyes   saw
what whitefolks   gave you to study
on me   the evening of your two room apartment
clutching your brown baby with silken black hair
to your chest she was fixed protected   from   me?

the long arm of your eyes leapt across the room
where your hand went up   making a wall of "no"
of "get back" I could not transcend

I was not from the government to reduce your food stamps
had no penis to penetrate your life
with blood of too many generations of solitudinal parenting
of grief disenfranchised   still
I frightened you

said you never encountered
a woman with a black face
in your own living room   without opening your mouth
asked what gruesome thing
I planned to do with you and your purring baby
without mumbling a word you asked   I answered
"love you" present   a gift   bed   for a baby

I wondered what you thought   as you chewed and swallowed
hoping your trepidation resolved   so you could finally taste
coconut and deep sweet molasses   cookies from my childhood
I could not tell you then   had never shared that morsel of my life before
can tell you now   have not shared it since
know   we can only do this together in a chair on high

still I see you   even as you do not look at me
my spirit is stronger than your diverting eyes

ARMED BY THE ANCESTORS

That which is the makeup of marrow
Is the sole content of my soul
The tidbit of Africa is the whole of Africa
The core of my being

Stolen ancestry
Is not the soul definer of
Who   how   what
One can be
Being as how
What and
Who speaks
Determines self
Enters the realm
Of a unified state of being
Cool
Hip
Downright flip
Fly
Introspection
In the face
Of rejection

Delving deep
To get
To the outside
Standing   guard
Guarding the soul
Content   of me
Being
As how I came to be Black
As a berry
Juice   Sweeter than
White cane
Which cannot
Produce
Color compared to black
Which can
And which can
Outcane
The cane sweetness of plain old sugar   *continues* ➹

Sweet love is the
Core of life in the universe
Which
When calculated
When rounded down
Then up again
Measures near Kelvin three
Astrophysics is fun for me

Black women
Who know the temperature of the universe
Are dangerous
Be careful
The
Questions
You ask
About
Qualifications
Might well put you at risk
Of exposure
To her
Knowledge

Ancestors come to me
Bearing gifts
Soft shell armor

Though I may be
Soft   spoken
Be
Ware
Razors are encased
In my tongue
Armed by the ancestors
In and from deep in the core of my continent
I am afraid
I could
Kill   that is
The true fear
Of my power
My rage

DEATH COMES FOR THOSE WHO CONTINUE LIVING

I am going to die
Will you come to my funeral?
Before it is too late to say goodbye?

Before I go
I want you to know
Will you Shiva for me?
Say what you know of me?
Sweet things
Taste of cakes and cookies
Sweets about me?
Sweetness of my life   a blessing to you?
Are you still sweet on me?

I am going to die
Will you come to my funeral?
Grieve for me
Mourn your loss of me
Rend your clothes for me?

Did you lose me?
If only you had paid closer attention
Would you not have lost me?
After you lost me
Did you not look hard enough to find me?
I will not be lost
You will not have lost me
I will be dead
Will you come to my funeral?

Will you walk around the block backward?
Will you tear your clothes for me?
Will you cover your mirrors for me?
Will you visit me?

continues ➷

I am going to die
Will you grace my grave with stones?
Lay me in the desert?
Let my bones absorb vitamin D?
Let the rains wash me?
Let the sands sift through my bones?
Will you be petrified?

Will you send me off with my favorite lyrics?
With my spoon   and comb and brush?

With three pomegranates?

I am going to die
You will   two
of us   eventually
So shall we live for now?

Shall we go for a ride on the sun?
Shall we sky dive?
Shall we sink into the deep of the blue green sea?
Shall we live?   Let's!

I am going to die
Will you come to my funeral?

Sherry Hardage

Sherry Hardage retired at 56 from a career designing electro-mechanical equipment for Los Alamos National Laboratory. She has written poetry since she was in high school, and won 2nd place and honorable mention in two national poetry contests. After retirement, she traveled the world for a few years until her mother's stroke brought her back to New Mexico. These poems reflect her life while traveling, caretaking, and surviving romance.

ANY PATH WILL DO

Pick a path dear friend,
I write to myself.
This is the same issue
we speak of every time
we talk.

Pick a path, any path.
It will shake you from
that frozen place where
you have lived forever
not living.

Pick a path with challenge.
For that one will be less
struggle than the constant
repetition of words you say
and say.

Pick a path. Break out.
You know exactly what
you face if you stay here.
Any path will do, paths
can change.

ENDLESS LOVE

As a young woman
I put all my eggs in the
Death Do We Part Basket.
He gambled and lost them.

Forever Passion came next.
A handsome devil who
threw them on the ground
while hunting prettier ones.

A bunch of eggs filled
a new wedding basket,
burnt crisp by jealousy.....
his child got more than he.

A thing is precious for its scarcity.
A whole basket is too many
for any one to have value,
or for any one to have.

These days I give single eggs
like manna from heaven.
All my friends get a few,
and the supply is endless.

MAGIC

Marimba music is a whirlwind
'round the gazebo.

A young man tries to teach
his fat girlfriend how to dance.

She prefers to look at her phone.
I want to scream at her.

Chica wake up and look in his eyes.
A handsome man wants to dance!

He wants you not someone else!
Believe what this old lady tells you.

In twenty years you'll remember
the night you learned to dance.

You won't remember one word
from those stupid messages.

Mentally berating the girl,
my body jives to the music.

A handsome *caballero* kisses
my hand and asks to dance.

We fly across the gazebo.
Laughing, falling, whirling.

Two hours later, he whispers
"me encanta" in my ear.

Then he bows, and I promise
to return the very next night.

OLD

Aging......an engaging project.
I remember being so much smarter.
Back when, on top of my game,
there was a sharp wit and fast mind.

Now I drive the speed limit.
Fear stairs for the potential fall.
Things far and close—out of focus
in every sense of the word.

Mornings I dread the aches
relieved by ibuprophen,
and floor exercises
to loosen swollen joints.

Never as a youth did I dream,
by the time I had enough
money and personal power,
I'd be too stiff to use it.

REGRETS

You were in love.
A little puppet
dangling from your
own heart strings.
She was the mistress
making you dance.
I got that.

It was a lovely day,
Valentine's day….
But then you said:
I'm spending the night
with her.
A knife to the heart,
twisted in pleasure.

It was Joanie you wanted
when you comforted me.
She was on your mind
when you called me her name.
Accidental knife twisting?
But you were in love.
I got that

Now you miss me
after all these years.
You're sorry you let her
dance you around.
You remember what
a great person I was.
I don't get that.

The ghost knife
spins insanely.
Long before Joanie,
you raped my child.
Long after you married,
she told me about it.
I was important to you?

continues ➹

I wasn't on that day.
I never intended
my daughter as
a bitch to satisfy
the eternal lust
of a hedonistic dog.
Fuck you.

Her words made the
world poker-hot white.
If there'd been a knife
I would have sliced you.
I apologized in tears.
Love had blinded me.
She got that.

Twenty five years
flew by in a second.
Joanie had enough.
Now you are old.
No pleasure in being
alone and lonely.
I get that.

You want us to
have coffee together?
An old-friend walk down
memory lane, lined
with the Valentine roses
I never received?
I get that too.

But no cup of coffee,
no number of flowers,
can make me forgive.
At the end of this life,
what I allowed you to do
will be my deepest regret.
Do you get that?

ALL MINE

Do I own this house?
By definition, yes.
I bought it. I paid for it.

Can it be taken from me?
Indeed. By war, a fire,
or government shenanigans.

Do I own this body—
marching around with my brain
that thinks I own both?

If I owned it, like a car,
I would fix it. New joints,
young eyes, taut skin.

If I truly owned this life
I would preserve it,
make it last forever.

Owning is a strange idea.
Even the oxygen I breathe
is borrowed from the Universe.

Yet knowing it is an illusion
changes nothing.
It's mine. All mine.

WHISKER

Instead of dashing out, he walked.
Quit leading down the stairs.
Stopped waking with the birds.

I knew our time was running out
but I never dreamed his back-end
could go dead in a day.

On Saturday I carried him,
held his back legs while he dove
into the grass for one last roll.

Still alert and purring,
I forced myself
to schedule his last hour.

GROWTH

I went with my friend,
her last trip to the doctor.

We viewed the x-rays.
Large clumps of tumors
attached by thin filaments
spread across the breadth.

Like viewing the earth at night
from a satellite advantage.
Clumps of cities run together,
attached by lighted roads.

Reality set in….
it's only a matter of time.

Wyatt H. Heard

In Memoriam
Judge Wyatt H. Heard • 1926-2017
Judge Heard's business card says much about him;

Judge, Arbitrator, Mediator, (Poet, clairvoyant — no extra charge)
Judge Heard spent much of his life in Houston Texas, in the law, as a lawyer, District Court Judge, and Mediator/Arbitrator. A profoundly deep thinker and spiritual person, he loved his God, his family, the western landscape, and Baylor Football.

Wyatt began writing poetry later in his life, shortly before moving from Houston, Texas to Albuquerque, New Mexico. In the Land of Enchantment, through sheer serendipity — a Folk Art Home Tour, and Wyatt's very observant wife enjoying a poem hung in the Brandt's home — he was invited by Richard Brandt to join the "Live Poets Society". 'Live Poets' provided support and community for Wyatt and his poetry from 1994 until his death. His most recent poems were shared at the Live Poet's meeting just two months before his death.

His favorite quote from Micah 6:8, sums up the values by which Wyatt led a long, useful life filled with love and humor:

> *"What does the Lord require of you?*
> *But to do Justice*
> *And to Love Mercy*
> *And to walk humbly with your God"*

SUNRISE

The mountains of Tao rise out of the earth reaching and yearning for the touch of light and life from the sun,

The valley below still in the shadows awaiting its turn for the sun to once again caress it, knowing it will occur in due time not trying to push its agenda —

Could I not learn like the valley to await God's design without injecting my own?

Will the sun rise in the east without my input?

As the gentle breeze flickers the poplar tree and the silver leaves shimmer to the first faint touch of the sun, the thought slowly emerges from the bowels of my center I am part of this event

Not larger nor smaller but just a part of the soil to which I will return!

SHADOW BOXING

That's what we do with our life! Instead of dealing with realities we dance around with the negative issues which are at our core from birth!

Why is it so difficult for us to face the truth? It takes a lot of grit to acknowledge what is real rather than the fantasy that floats in our brain!

If we take an honest inventory of the issues floating in our cerebellum then God can help guide us to a plateau which embellishes to have a sound connection with the heavenly realm!

We have all been on this journey since birth and God will not allow us to falter.

EFFICIENCY

How long did it take for God to raise up the mountains,
a million or two years? Maybe more?

I look at the elm outside my window with a few dead branches,
with my limited tools—arms and legs, I could more efficiently
trim that tree today

God may send a strong wind and trim out the lifeless limbs
but it may be a year or two!

Does this make God the more inefficient? Are my arms and legs
more efficient than God's weapons?

Is God's concept of time different than mine? Or maybe as the
old covenant expresses it—a thousand years is but a day to the
father—mother of us all.

Man measures time by the hour glass and therefore efficiency
occurs within a span which our minds can comprehend—

Agelessness and timelessness are not only foreign to us but
maybe beyond our reach?

CHURCH

We dress up in our best and polish our shoes, it is important to look our best. Why?

Is church about our fractured lives? If so, why do we attempt to portray the opposite—that which is not real?

Is denial so strong in our system that we are afraid of the truth?

Are we so threatened with our weaknesses?

Shall we not live by the Ethiopian proverb "He who conceals his disease cannot be cured?"

Is it not the thrust and central theme of the New Covenant the brokenness of Jesus of Nazareth?

The message at the service today was "Killing in Ireland in the name of God"—is that not insanity?

As I sit in church the overwhelming urge is to Prostrate my body and soul before the altar and plead:

Father—Mother to us, all come and heal the basement of my life.

BENJAMIN

There he comes across the snow
crossing the athletic field
that funny gait like Larry's
where he kicks out his left foot

I am waiting in the car
to take him to the airport
I won't have him much longer
before college — realizing
I do not "own" him
he's a gift!

He is the "son" but his effect
on me has been profound
as I gaze across the field
watching him trudge through the snow
knowing he will be in my vehicle
in about thirty seconds
the shortness of the lapsed time
is indicative in a larger scale
of the brief time we have left
before college

Be grateful for what you
have left and try to use it
knowing the brevity is a reality

Life is a series of small pin points
of time when the direction of life
is flooded with options and
we are hopeful
our compass will strike true north
so as not to lose our way

My encounter with him in the
"Sun-Set" of life pushes me
around like a huge beach ball
but I know I have connected
with him and we have exchanged
the glue of life

RIO

Rio purchased November 26, 1999
from Mona Lisa Gonzales (if you please)

New saddle bridle   and blanket
after some weeks he began to pitch
and act agitated

Consultation—maybe saddle does not fit
this high withered thoroughbred sixteen hands
a McClellan saddle the answer
and the General knew his horses
he didn't believe he was as smart as Bobby Lee
which was probably correct
but Grant knew he was not as smart as Lee
but he knew it did not matter
since he had more men and material and would win

Maybe Rio has a lot of horse sense
to know what does not work for him
and figured a way to communicate this need
maybe all of us could use more horse sense like Rio

ODE TO HEIDI

She is related to
    the ocean
she is a descendant of
    its sound and
        movement

It seems as water
    has chosen her as
    an acolyte

She is a part of the
    rolling lineage
of the waves and the
    tide is eternal in
her as she moves to
    bridge the gulf
    between relationships
with others and her
    God

The history of water
    has entered her
    because it was
passed from mother
to child in our
    beginnings

She leaned into
    sound of the ocean
to remember God is
    not mute
and is connected to
    her eternally

She works with
    The ferocity
Of one from the
    South who has
    waded the Rio
    Grande

She teaches us all
    (her extended family)
how to manage
    this world and
    probably the
    next

Georgia Jones-Davis

Georgia Jones-Davis grew up in Northern New Mexico and Southern California. A former free-lance journalist and *Los Angeles Times* Assistant Book Editor, her poetry has appeared in *West Wind, The California Quarterly, Brevities, The Bicycle Review, Nebo, Eclipse, poetic diversity, Ascent Aspiration* and *South Bank Poetry*. She served on the board of Valley Contemporary Poets, a Southern California non-profit; she was honored as one of the 2010 Newer Poets by the Los Angeles Poetry Festival and the Public Library Aloud Series. She is the author of two chapbooks, *Blue Poodle* (2011) and *Night School* (2015), published by Finishing Line Press. Georgia lives in Santa Fe, NM.

SUNDAY MORNING LA

Birds singing. Mud winter
in the Irish green
of lavish avocado trees,
in swaying date palms.

These old LA hills
are steep jungles,
tight concrete streets,
gardens of yellow and blue
craftsmen cottages, red tiled
noir era Spanish.

The thoughts of houses sliding
into the sea recede.
Those swept away
were old money.
So sad, oh well, there's nothing.

Here, near downtown, lovers
croon behind papery walls.
Such soft laughter brings babies
and breakfast,
toast soldiers dipped
into runny eggs in china cups.

And Echo Park is a party
on a hot January day.
A marching band of brown kids,
laborers on a day off fishing the lake,
water you would want to never drink.

A very few geese and ducks,
every designer dog in LA on a leash,
every hipster from Nebraska
with an agent parading.

continues ➤

LA's pretty flag
never to fly higher.
The sun kisses the soft skin
of Hollywood's children.
At Intelligentsia the hot coffee
is fruit forward as wine.

My daughter's life here
opens like an invitation.
Roses and iris and peonies
tumble into her hands.

She gathers the drooping beauties
from her friend's pop-up flower stand,
blooms orphaned after
some music video shoot.

My daughter hugs
their lingering perfume
to her still widening heart.

GOING NOWHERE

People live far apart here,
the girl notices from the car.
Mom, dad, the girl, leave LA,
drive the Chevy north
through the San Joaquin Valley.
They pass onion fields, cattle, dirt roads
that veer off into vast ranches.

You can play the piano after ten
in these parts, jokes dad.
Mom, behind cat-eyed sunglasses,
smiles that smile that says
I'm not happy.

Dad calls on his customers
in Fresno, Visalia. The horse people
aren't buying today.
At dusk they reach Modesto,
a motel with a twinkling pool
beneath a pink neon flamingo.

They eat dinner at The Great Wall.
The girl feels so grown-up
sipping hot tea,
using a finger bowl.
The fortune cookies are stale.

Neat squares of beds
with rough sheets
wait for them in a blue room
with dizzy paintings of flowers.
The girl likes the emptiness,
the drunk-looking paintings,
drawers with a Gideon bible
and nothing else.

continues ➴

She likes how the street lights
spill through the white blinds,
the night full of unknown voices,
whoosh of cars,
growls of trucks.

In the morning someone else
has to make their beds.
At breakfast, the toast soggy but good.
Mom pours some of her coffee
into the girl's frosted glass of milk
and dangles a Salem cigarette.
Dad pays and loads up the Chevy.

The motel vanishes in a pink blur.
The girl watches how
the flat world speeds up
as if the valley
were on wheels
and the girl, her mother and father,
the ones standing still.

From *Night School*

MONUMENTAL DOG

Where is the dog the Soviets
shot into space in 1957?
Where is Laika tonight?
Her bones could be sailing overhead,
a satellite of the Cold War
stuck in the traffic of the commuting sky.
Experts now contend
that she died of overheating
within hours of launch
because her RJ sustainer failed
to separate from the payload.
She died,
the rest of us believe,
an orbiting, kenneled cosmonaut,
a terrified Dog Star,
night and day chasing past her,
the full moon escaping fast as a cat.
She howled, "I am the only dog circling
the campfire of the world,
lonesome as a wolf lurking
in prehistoric shadows."
On the sixth day her breath evaporated.
She starved and froze in her capsule
as the human sounds she recalled—
"Moya Malishka, moya Laylika"—
receded in her ears
with the memory of meat
and Kremlin bells only a dog can hear.
Laika was mailed into space,
a letter never answered,
a missal to the gods of the future.
She submitted to her handler's
velvet-voiced commands, to please
the same voice that whispered her name.
She thrilled to the clammy, cushiony hands
that stroked her fur
even as they strapped her in.

From *Night School*

MISSING DON HO

When I was eighteen I traveled to Hawaii
with a tribe of old and holy women from the Midwest.

I wore a tight yellow sheath, tasted papaya for the first time.
My roommate slept in curlers, studied her bible before bed.

Midnight I was down on the beach stepping into the heart-breaking
breakers that rolled beneath a yellow ukulele moon.

Those hot nights in Oahu how Don Ho filled the churchy, starchy hearts
of the sturdy *wahinis* from the islands of Iowa and Indiana and Illinois

with naughty hulas and pineapple dreams. The lingering "aloooooha"
of Don Ho was what the fat, widowed, moo-mooed belles took home

to deep lakes and wide rivers, corn and wheat fields of the Sandburg prairie
that rolled like an ocean beneath a yellow ukulele moon.

From *Blue Poodle*

LAST NIGHT

All night the house groans,
dishes sigh beneath
their stoneware weight.

Lights off, you stare
into the fireplace,
the flat screen of crackling,

hiss and spit—the devil
that eats memory and ambition;
radio tuned to classical,

a symphony from Riga or Latvia,
some eastern black hole of the war.
The strings are mad with loss.

Beyond the fire the darkness inhales
and exhales. Before you know it,
years have passed.

From *Night School*

Sheila Ortego McLaughlin

Sheila Ortego McLaughlin is President Emeritus of Santa Fe Community College and author of *The Road from La Cueva,* a first place winner for novels in the 2008 New Mexico Book Awards. She lives in Corrales, New Mexico, and continues to write, focusing on poetry and historical fiction.

VALENTINE

I chop with blunt-nose scissors
Thick red paper
Paste in a jar, so sweet
I can eat it
Doily, snowflake white
Glitter in a plastic tube
spilling silver

I hold it behind my back
in sticky fingers
paste still wet

Teacher turns to look
the other way
I put it on your desk
then run
Fat, heart-shape candy
Pale pink, chalk-sugar
melts on my tongue
"Be Mine"

I jump on the swing set
Push off, swing high
heart pounding
I have done it!
I have given my heart to you!

After the bell rings
I find on my desk
a box of paper valentines
from you

Teacher said one for each girl in class
But my name is on every one

TIGER

You swing your arms
walking on sunshine
so tall, the trees shimmer below
and clouds circle your head

Everything is wrapped up
tied in a shiny bow
I hang on your waist
like Curious George
and You like the Man in the Yellow Hat

And just when all is right with the world
this god-damned tiger
leaps from undergrowth
knocks you down
starts gnawing on your leg

One funny thing I notice
is that the tiger is smiling
He has you!!
He glances up to see if you're writhing
but there's not much pain
and no blood to speak of

You peel him off
and lean over to inspect the wound
It's about 8 inches long
enough to warrant stitches
He watches from the sidelines
Still smiling, Cheshire-like

MOTHER'S LITTLE GARDEN

I pulled the weeds today
Borrowing my mother's grief to dodge my own
Now more clear are the married roses
The Ruby, small and pale, for my grandmother
The John Franklin, tall and vibrant, for my grandfather

Ruby struggled with the transplant
Just as my mother will
in this new home where the two have followed her
They fade, resist, then miraculously
bloom in profusion

There stands the Indian Hawthorne
struggling to thrive
Beset by crabgrass and goatheads
Yet still, bearing new leaves, persistent

I think of my husband's illness and his will
to live, to survive

Here, mother's fountain
with new strawberries all around
offering themselves up
in flower, and fruit

We lift them to our lips in thanks
that we grow here
weedy, brambled and thirsty
but still in the sweetness of living

THE SURFACE OF THE WATER

I want to climb your glass mountain
in iron shoes
be your girl, your elfin-maid
your wild woman

I want to travel to the surface of the earth
pass through rocks and walls
fly in the air
to you

I want to meet you at the water dance
be your stolen lady, your wood maid, your water nymph

We could play on the surface of the water
dance in the moonlight on velvet grass
sing with voices like silver bells
sleep in a green meadow
with garlands of flowers in our hair

LOT 211: ARTIFACTS FROM POMPEII

A wine bottle with figure of Bacchus
Braziers for use outdoors in balmy weather
Golden earrings and implements for the bath
The chain used for a guard dog that struggled for air
    as the ash fell down
    until the chain had reached its end
The shackles that bound a slave
    who hobbled his way to the gates
    until fire descended to take him
The Fresco paintings of manicured gardens
The lamp from a brothel
The remains of a marbled floor
The comb from a servant's room
Assembled here for your perusal
    for your consideration
    reminders, if you will
Of life sublime
Of life debased
Of suffering
Of death, Who comes for all

OPENING

When light falls
on petals of rose
soft as lamb's belly
perfume drunk with itself
that is only the half of it

The other half is shadow,
creased, hidden places

I breathe in
The scent of you catches
like a thorn
The air is heady,
hot and sweet
the sound of you velvet

My petals open
arc upward
honey rises in my throat
to you

SKINNING A CAT

Peeling this part of our love away
must be like skinning a cat

There's a lot of yowling and scratching
bloodletting, really

And then things get real quiet
You've got a handful of bone and muscle

And a pool of blood
(the cat's and yours)

And suddenly you wonder why you did it
You miss the little bugger

But it's too late

THE BIG BANG

I felt my heart would explode
and collapse upon itself
like a black hole

The big bang
hanging over us like a threat

While one kiss
destroyed the universe
and created a million new

LEAVING

our leaving was
just a sliding apart of fingers

but the air stretched tight
between us
and all the miles that we passed through
and the tension pulls on my skin
in the direction of you

Rheta Moazzami

Though Rheta Moazzami identifies as a writer and musician at her core, her interests and history have run the gamut. She has written for a small town newspaper, a local magazine, her company newsletter; and she has been published in *The Sun* magazine. But, that's only the writing. Don't get her started about the biotech company she represents that can mitigate aging.

She believes music and poetry are integrally related. She has played for a country and western band, is currently pianist for a church, is a member of both a piano group that plays for each other, and a trio of piano, cello and violin.

She holds an MPA with an emphasis in Environmental Policy and is most recently credentialed in Personal Care and Support.

COY MOON

Coy moon, do not flirt with me tonight!
I have miles to roll,
Red tail lights to attend,
And minute details to perfect.

I tell you fat, silver slice
I have no time for mystery,
For I am busy and important.

Do not tempt me to pull over
And bathe in your beams.

Know my soul longs to
Lose myself in your light,
Relinquish the world to
Rejoice in our unity!

But, I have no time.
For I am busy and important.

VICTIM—NOT INVICTUS

Lest your younger brother
Or your son think you a hero
And want to follow you,
Let us call you Victim.

Though brave you may have been
And worthy of compassion,
Dying does not a hero make.
Dying at eighteen
A tragic waste makes.

Let us instead remember you
By staying mindful as we use
The gas and oil
You spilled your blood for.

FROM THE NURSING HOME

Eight-eleven

Are we married?
No. I don't want to be married. I like being single.
I just want to go to Albuquerque.
Well, Baby, we'll go, says he.
How we gonna go?
We'll just get on down the road.
Can you get out of that chair and come sit beside me?
O.K. But, I just want to go to Albuquerque.
We'll go, Baby, by God we'll go!
How we gonna go?
We'll just make tracks outta here.
You wanna go to the room?
O.K. What's our room number?
I don't know. I'll go ask the nurse.
She wheels like the roadrunner—full speed ahead.
Eight-eleven. She wrote it down.
Well, let's skeedaddle out of here.

Where's Edie? I ask the next day.
They moved her to the locked ward, except they say the *memory unit.*
Why?
She was wheeling into people's rooms.
Now he wheels the halls.
Where's my room?
Eight-eleven, everyone says at once.

ARE YOU A MOTHER?

Help! I hear from the hall.
She is frustrated and desperate,
Tangled in sheets and bedclothes.
Over crepey husks of breasts
I pull and straighten,
Smooth the covers,
Stroke her face,
Lean down and kiss her forehead.

She looks up and tells me how pretty I am,
Then lapses into German I don't understand.

Next day, in her rubber-soled socks,
She inches in her wheelchair all afternoon,
Her poetry coloring the air:
You got a big, shitty hiney,
And your titties ain't so pretty!

In the dining room I bend down to her.
She draws back in fear.
We're friends, I say.
She grins and asks the question
She always asks me now,
Are you a mother?

'TIL DEATH

He had his own company, flew his own plane,
Lived the American dream.
Raised a lovely family. Still has the pictures.

Confused after an injury,
Said lovely family has him declared incompetent,
Leaves him in the nursing home.

Sixty-six years we've been married, he says.
Sixty-six years. I know we were in love.
And I thought it was 'til death do us part.

Shari Morrison

Shari Morrison's mother was a poet as well as mother to thirteen children. The youngest of the 13, Morrison learned about her mother's poems only after she'd published her first book, *Selected Writings From Taos* in 1996. Now she considers herself a "second generation" poet.

The beauty of nature has long been a muse for Morrison, as have the personalities of characters that she's met. An upcoming book titled *Poetry at 90 MPH* features snapshots of chocolate bars of railroad cars speeding along, wildflowers merging onto the highway and grandfather Ponderosa pines minding their families. Her caricatures of people come alive for the reader in short poems, which were written by hand in her car, as she traveled the long stretches of highway in the Southwest as publisher of *Art Talk Newspaper*.

Morrison currently is a Contributing Editor for *Western Art & Architecture Magazine*.

ODE TO A SWAN

It was only a moment, maybe two or more
That captured me and held me its prisoner
For all that day, and the next and the next.

So slowly, and elegantly I have never been seized.
It was the power in the beauty of a single swan that
Overpowered me, its regal neck a gesture

Of grace and dignity in a roadside pond filled
With common ducks and geese, who could
Never capture one's attention like the smooth

White feathers of the swan, the sun lighting them
Like a rare treasure, newly found, and who with ease,
Swept its legs backwards and swam the circle of pond.

FOR A TIME

For a time we did sup—
He and I.
From lips that were
Supple and willing,
I tasted his sweetness
And he tasted mine.

We were seeking that
Which joins two
Making them into one.

Passions flowed,
Gently coaxing
Us into love.

Relishing each other,
We savored each
Morsel of touch,
Delighted in each
Knowing glance.

Then he was gone,
No where
To be found—

THAT OCTOBER DAY

That day, my soul was so giddy,
The only word
I breathlessly spoke
Was WOW!

Quick intakes of breath
Around each curve
Fed my lungs oxygen
Needed at 10,000 feet.

As my heart swelled
With awe, my eyes
Reached out to touch
Each golden leaf,
　　　　Each smooth white
　　　　Trunk of Aspen tree.

We met somewhere
In the deep blue of the sky
Between us and hugged
Like long lost relatives.

As the sun moved
Across the Colorado sky
And danced upon the tree tops,
I wanted to lay a table

continues ➚

With the finest feast
Amongst the forest
And live there forevermore,
Preserving, like a good jam,

Every tasty morsel
That had settled
On the tongues of my eyes
And the tongues of my soul.

I was giddy like a child,
Wanting to run around
Catching leaves in midair.
I wanted to wallow in a
      Huge pile of Golden yellow.

I was
Totally,
Recklessly,
Helplessly
In love
      On that October day.

DREAMS

What happens to dreams unfulfilled?
Do they gather together
One upon another
Until they make a mountain tall?

Or do they drift about
In and out of reality
Until they settle on the ground
Creating fields of possibilities?

A friend dreamed for years
Of a little white cottage with
A white picket fence
Sitting at the ocean's edge.
       But grapes and smoke took their toll

And wiped the dream slate clean.
Now she lives in a world
Where dreams are mixed
With anxieties, not
       Understanding, which is which?

So where is her dream now?
Is it up amongst the clouds?
Does it exist in part or whole
For someone else to grab and hold?

Mimi Rhodes

M. Verlaine Rhodes (Mimi) was born and raised in Nyack, New York, on the Hudson. She is a fourth generation artist, and holds an MFA from the *Instituto Allende, Universidad de Guanajuato, Mexico.* She married Robert Rhodes in St. Petersburg, Florida. Among their long adventures together, she became the mother of their five children. She began writing poetry in 2013 when, inspired by her husband, Bob, she joined the Live Poets' Society.

SAVE ME A PLACE

I saw the face of my grandchild Eli
In a clip of a film at the Holocaust Museum
Among little children being loaded on the bus
That would take them to the camp
Too many small hands out open bus windows
Happily fluttering their goodbyes
Like small white birds that are heavenly bound

I saw a bin of women's and children's shoes
Uniformly made gray
By earth, time and sorrow
Color of ashes

Save me a place at the Wailing Wall

SHROUDED ROOMS OF MEMORY

Shrouded rooms of memory
Clear at night in dreams
A barefoot woman passed me by
On a street in Mexico
Her face so beautiful, so young
Her garments so tattered and worn
A cloth over her raven black hair
Winding down around a baby
She held to her breast
Her dark eyes fixed straight ahead
A look of peace on her face
Or was it resignation?
I passed her by then turned to look
I wanted to find her again,
Give her money to buy some shoes.

I walked until the street turned dust
Following footsteps traced in sand
Passed by a man with hollow eyes
Lying in my path
But she had disappeared
And I had gone too far.
My vision began to blur
My feet too I saw were bare
Colors on walls before my eyes
Sienna, ochre and tan,
Melting in the boiling sun,
Puddling in the sand.
She was a Madonna in a ragged dress;
I was lost in an ancient land.

LUNCH WITH MOTHER TERESA

He was a business man
Traveling in India
When he saw her at an airport,
A sister on either side
She was smaller than pictures had implied
Yet there was an energy about her
A purpose to her stride.

He went up to her and told her
How much he admired her work
"I wanted to be a priest," he said
My family was against it."
They spoke and she gave him an invitation
"Would you like to come to lunch on Tuesday?"
"I'd be honored," he said, he'd give her a generous donation
To aid her in her mission,
Savoring telling his friends
He had lunch with Mother Teresa.

On that appointed day
He found himself in a warehouse district in old Bombay
"No restaurant here," he said
"No mistake," the driver said
"There's the number on the wall."

When he opened the large wooden door,
He saw a room full of people on pallets
Lying on the floor
"I'm glad you came," she said.
"Let me show you how.
Here's the caldron and the ladle.
There the bowls upon the table."

She showed him how to lift and cradle each person
How to bring the bowl to their lips
So they could drink the soup
"The look of gratitude in each person's eyes," he said
"Changed my life forever."

MEMORY OF FLIGHT

Feeling the lightness of her ethereal being
And lured by the cries of the seabirds,
She trailed her long brown hair
In the blue green Coral Sea
Letting it follow the contours of the reef
Until it snagged on the rocks below
Pulling her downward
Tethering her to the Earth.
That was long ago
Her hair bleached white by the brine of the sea,
Her wings no more than a membrane now,
She drifts and tangles with seaweed and kelp.
When the water is a roiling swell
She rides the waves to the shore
And is pulled seaward again.
Afternoons she gazes at the heavens
Marveling at the shapes the clouds will take
And the nuances of color in the ethereal skies.
When the moon is full
Avenues of light on the water
Beckon her home
Memory of flight dissolving as in a dream,
Air, space and lightness into liquid form

COTTON CANDY
(for my brother)

Out from the northern winter
Leaving snowsuits and galoshes behind
We arrived in the land of eternal summer
Our parents together; a new beginning.
Do you remember nights at the tennis courts,
Overhead lights and the sound of motorized planes
Circling at the end of wires,
I, holding onto my childhood
Racing you to the highest point on our swings?
Only gravity held us back.
Do you remember walking to the pavilion
At the end of the pier,
The smell of the bay
Carried on warm tropical breezes,
Music and the lights on the water,
Frozen custard cones and cotton candy
That evaporated in our mouths,
Our parents together happy?
We didn't know then that it couldn't last forever.
    Our parents' marriage
        our happiness
            our youth.

RUN

It was open hunting season
The thrill of the hunt,
The hunter for his prey
Was steadily moving him on

The prey knows when it's being followed,
When it's being stalked,
The voice of the other,
The mate, the mother,
"Run," she tells it, "Run!"

Running, a sign of fear
Only excites the hunter more
The prey no match for the hunter's gun
Instinct says to run

He was a different kind of prey
"Home of the free, land of the brave"
He would stand his ground.
"Why you followin' me?"

A scream rang out
A shot from a gun
A bullet to the heart
Another unarmed youth
Lay dead upon the ground

Another mother's son
Nineteen years of nurturing
"Run," she said, "Run!"

The president said,
"If I had a son
He'd look a lot like Trayvon."
"Run," she said, "Run!"

The killer was found innocent
Because he was afraid
"American justice" on trial
"Run," she said, "Run!"

Robert Rhodes

Robert Rhodes has been a technical writer, a teacher, an editor, director of a museum, and a major figure in the Live Poets' Society. He was born in South Carolina, attended the University of Florida, UNM, and has an M.A. and a Ph.D. He lives with his wife in Santa Fe, writes poems and walks his dog.

LION DREAMING

I am a lion dreaming
At home among elephants

I raise my massive head
In full grasp of the plain

Blood dries on my muzzle
From the fresh kill before me

When I open my jaws to roar
More blood drips from my rough, red tongue

My comely lioness arrives
To feed on parts I leave for her

I give her golden rump a swat
Which she's permitted to ignore

Nothing moves before I look
Without permission of my eyes

Not wind to blow, nor bird to fly
Not river to run, nor sun to rise

I wake up from lion dreaming
Caged by time in an old man's mind

YOU THINK THIS NEW SHAPE WILL PROTECT YOU

You think this new shape will protect you?
Come confess that you are witches still.
Must another million burn to teach you
Not to make a weapon of your brooms?

You send your spirits to trouble sleep
Disturbing fortune in her bedsheets
But we have cures for this affliction
Courts to dispossess for madness sake.

Take counsel of your possession, ladies,
Keep to the shape that God has given you
Lest sense should overreach desire
And you be less that you suppose.

What have we denied you, ladies?
Come confess and we'll forgive you.
What have we denied you, witches
That you take so long to burn?

APOSTLE OF CREDIT

How can a man get out of a pink car
And expect to be taken seriously?
With his black coat and smiling face,
You know he's out to take you.
His moist and too eager hand
Fumbles and pumps at yours;
You are being primed, my friend.
Beware the flow of coin
That presently starts to run
From dry pockets with holes
That held nothing but your hands.
Before this magician in a pink car
Lays the world out at your feet.
This modern Mephistopheles
Has bargained for your soul,
Nor will your damnation
Be any less complete
Than were it dreamed up
Some dark midnight hour
In a castle by the Rhine,
Though now they call it credit
And the devil wears a tie.

QUICKER THAN THE EYE

We knew the rabbit was a fake
And the lovely lady wore a padded bra.
We knew words had nothing to do
With turning silk scarves into birds.
Our hot eyes quick to catch deception,
We caught the secret of the saw.
Getting wiser we found how he walked
Through two doors of stainless steel,
How he climbed a staircase that wasn't there
And upright in the air appeared to smile.
But not until the mirror broke,
Did we see ourselves be folded,
Put away with other props
And carried off in paper boxes.

———————————

Pull the curtain back
Dawn is ready to begin
Hurry to your seats.

TALES OF THE DEEP

Nautically speaking
Things that make love in the sea
Are naughty indeed.
I give you the squid
Thrusting his tentacle deep
Down the throat of his love,
Bursting with his squidish sperm
Causing such panic
That she breaks off the affair,
Spitting out his offering
Which forms a snaky serpent
Unable to reproduce
With others of its kind,
A real sea serpent
Angry at its creation
Denying its own creators
Both male and female;
Neutered creature if you will
Deeply removed from acts of love.

VENTURING DOUBT

Across the bridges burnt in my escape
A doubt that comes in constant changing shape
Is that I've left behind unjustified
A venturing urge I might have better tried.
Neglected in my hurried try for shore
To drown awhile and trust the water more,
Found land too soon to spend more time at sea
And planting flags made no discovery
Vague lands where doubt is more divine
And thought itself the capitol of wine
With cause divorced by law from all that's real
And difference an absolute ideal
Where poets write on walls iambic truth
And every sayer's guaranteed his sooth,
Where wise are wise in simple sympathy
And torches burn to mark this mystery
But all such ventures end for me in stress
With a terrible urging to confess
That I've drifted by chance upon a beach
A shell that serves to store a doubtful reach.

Sally Anne Rosenberg

When I was five years old, my teacher asked me to count to ten. When I got to 4, I said to the teacher, "I can't remember the name of the number but 1 plus 3 makes that number, and 6 take away 2 makes that number."

She interrupted me then and said, "If you don't know the names you don't know the numbers."

I've spent most of my adult life teaching high school mathematics and looking for words that describe thoughts, feelings, actions, the world in more than one simple word. There are many names for any number, and each name gives a different perspective and different information. Finding those words that give as much to the non-number words is hard for me. Words don't come easily.

But when they come, there is a great joy and, if I'm lucky, a poem.

GRASSES

Spring grasses
Brighten
Dull winter woods

Summer grasses
Swallow
Bright spring flowers

Autumn grasses
Bleach
Green summer hills

Winter grasses
Stiffen
Making bad beds

JANUARY 8, 2005

In a lantern — a lit candle
Mist softens the flame
Heavy rains can't dampen the light

Morning becomes noon — noon, evening
The mist, the rain and the flame continue
Long, long into the night

Finally, you blow the candle out
The flame is gone —
Leaving

The mist, the rain and you

EARLY MORNING FORECAST

The crescent moon and I
watch the sun rise,
bringing dappled sunshine
to the canyon's floor.

The geraniums keep their red
all night.
The unexpected purple flowers
open only to the sun.

It's going to be hot today.

The moon will travel on
and find a new night,
the purple ones will close in
upon themselves.

But the geraniums and I,
we will wilt
in the withering sun
until it sets and night descends.

YIN AND YANG

Sunny morning, rainy afternoon.
A morning hike, an afternoon book.
We were to go to dinner,
But my calls go unanswered.
The rains and the book go on into the night.

THE RISING MOON

Sitting on the deck
Waiting for the moon to rise
I think of you, my new friend.
Both of us alone tonight
Happy in our quietness, our solitude.

I wonder are you too
Waiting for the sunset
So the moon can rise
In all its bright, round glory?

It's getting dark and my eyes
Aren't what they used to be.
I light a candle to see.
Engrossed in my writing
I look up in time to see
The whiteness peaking above the hill.
I blow out the candle and
Wait for the moon.

There's a hole in the trees
At the top of the hill
The moon pokes through
Until it escapes
And begins its nightly walk
Across the sky.

My friend,
This poem was meant for you,
But the moon got top billing.

I suspect you'll understand.

THE CHANGING NEIGHBORHOOD

Delores's coffee shop is gone.
Even the little Italian place
Will soon be a memory.
Now the restaurants are
Thai, Sushi, Ecuadorian.
It's hard to find
macaroni and cheese
meatloaf and gravy
spaghetti and meatballs.
no wonder I became
A vegetarian.

AN A FOR AN A

He was fourteen
and too short for his feet.
He wrote of suicide
while drawing dancing figures
and playing Macbeth.
The suicide was bloody.
In the movie he used
gallons of ketchup.
In class he was quiet.
He always got B minuses
and wrote poetry
on the back of his homework.

At sixteen
he'd grown into his feet.
He wouldn't speak of the movie
and would only say
he'd been through his suicide.
He was still quiet in class.

He began to get A's.
His poems he kept to himself.

ALMOST HAIKU

I

The steaming coffee
Sitting on the table
Had no one to drink it

II

Running for the bus
Mother and daughter laugh
As the bus pulls away

AFTER NOT WRITING FOR A LONG TIME

It's been too long.
Words bang and crash into each other
Not knowing where to go.
The long ones trip over themselves.
The short ones bump around and over
The sounds and meanings
Of what I'm trying to say.
Some have lost their music and their tenor.
Others are just plain lost.
I listen and wait, until I finally hear a word
Struggling to be heard.

ON WRITING A STORY

letters fall off the page
they fly across the floor
jump out the window
onto the wind

outside the wind whispers
but i don't know what it's saying
listening for the words
the lost letters make
takes more effort
than I seem to have

back inside i write on the computer
hoping the letters will stay put
they don't
they jump off the screen just as easily

the days, the weeks pass
a few letters hold together
a word
a phrase

until finally
when i turn my back
the letters stay put
and
the story begins

ON SEEING MY COUSIN WHEN WE TURNED SIXTY

Living many miles away
Our paths seldom cross.
But today we walked the mountains.
The sun keeping us warm
While the wind blew cold.

You smiled telling me tomorrow
You'd be alone in your tent
Smoking a cigar, enjoying a cup of wine.
You frowned about being sixty,
Grey hair and appearing wrinkles.

Sixty is easier on me.
I resent the jump in insurance costs,
Sore knees from the mountain hike,
And being knocked out by 2 beers.

But then,
You always could drink more than I.

A LAZY SUNDAY MORNING CONVERSATION

I don't remember what we said.
Not that it matters.
We were just together
Driving down Sunset.
You had your white shirt
And sports jacket on,
And proud Mama thought—
How handsome you are.

Then we rounded a bend
And there was Mt. Baldy
White from the first snow.
The two of us wanting to skip the day
And head for them thar hills.
Instead we kept going
The conversation and lulls
Keeping time with the traffic.

Suddenly, we were at your place—
A hug, a kiss and the conversation ended,
But not Mama's smile nor Baldy's snow.

WHEN WE WERE YOUNG

Back when we were new I used to think
We had a secret truth, you and I.
A truth that few had known
And fewer yet could sing.
But now I wonder—
"Truth" is a mighty word
And one whose meaning is not so easily found.
The joy of us was mystical as were
The touches and the kisses that filled our days.
But mystery and truth are not the same
And though I see the mystery in us still
I must admit the "secret truth" escapes me.
And what I find is you and I entwined
Into an us that is and only is.

Michael Woodruff

Michael L. Woodruff is a graduate of the Writer's Workshop with a Fine Arts degree from the University of Nebraska at Omaha. Recipient of Riekes Scholarship for writing and author of *This is the Moon*, a collection of short stories. Currently he is the organizer of a Writer's Workshop in Albuquerque NM.

GLASS SEA (REVELATIONS 15)

Hid in stoic shadows, hands feign lust
to escape the joyous harps of Moses Song,
and not a humbled one among the throng,
save a lamb mixing mercy in the dust.

If Hades could breathe sweet, jaded rebukes
tears would whisper a nuance
to these desolate vessels and chance
a row of sixes between their ears.

Then I could swim through this glass sea,
cut by a fallen flame, shards all,
but better to temper familiar whims
in times when sacred seas seem so small.

MARBLES

During recess,
boys sit along the concrete,
toe to toe,
with marbles between their legs,
and shout:
"Peeries!"
"Steelies!"
"Boulders!"
Hands sweat ready
to shoot the cat-eyes
into the crotch
of these wide-eyed entrepreneurs,
while little girls
scratch their heads
and wonder why
little boys act so silly.

ONE

People say:
There is one in every crowd;
And I tell myself:
I must be that one
they are talking about,
because I feel the separation
they see.
I am one of a kind,
at any given time,
in any given space.
I stand out,
an unwanted presence.

The world is filled with ones
crowding the psychology
of our daily lives.
So, you are the one for me,
clarity without reason,
a perfect declaration
of ownership, or
one is as good as another,
a vague indifference
brought about by impatience, or
one is as one does,
to each his own,
a declared drama
I continue to re-visit.

continues

They are the ones,
caught,
and as guilty as a sin,
hiding,
flashed by a blinding light.
But they are not the only ones,
mind you,
but a pocket full of ones,
destined for a scrutiny
that attempts to divert attention
from every ones only fear.

There is only one way,
my way,
or the highway,
which really means two ways,
forcing a convergence
to a singular road,
a consolidation of will.
How about this one
for the road
-a toast,
to settle the clarity
of this single resolve.

I need to get one thing straight,
In my mind,
At least,
as straight as one can get,
drawing the line,
freehand,
from point to crooked point,
with an empty quill.

continues ✐

It is always one thing,
at one time,
in one great moment,
fixed in eternal stress,
that needs to be straightened out.
Multi-tasking is a myth
created to strangle my confidence.

One man's myth is another man's truth,
and there is nothing wrong
with getting your wisdom
from one silent stone,
provided you believe it is true.

I'd like to claim a monogamy
in my attentions concerning all my ones.
But, one thing is for certain,
I have gathered my distractions
in disturbing abundance,
from one source or another.

I collect each one, as they come,
together with other ones,
one after another,
good ones, bad ones,
to create one big bundle,
to set my head on,
to sleep,
my only substance,
and then, finally,
I find ways to apply each
to my solitary life.

SITTING ON THE CHURCH STEPS IN MAYETTA, KANSAS

Imagine my surprise,
when slapped in the face
for slipping a hand around
to touch the forbidden arch,
all cotton, all soft,
And a sharp echo
bounces off the doors
of the church like a warning.

A choir of crickets,
hiding in the night laugh,
and I blush.
The concrete cools my pants,
and I watch her hands strain,
folding the corners
of her pocket bible,
back and forth
to weaken the pages.

I can see only shadows,
like in Plato's cave,
across the street,
images
jagged against the dark sky.
Without the moon

everything is black,
except a dusty street lamp
fighting the chaotic flicker
of moths and gnats.

A sudden wind pushes
against the old church,
and narrow windows,
cracked with age,
give me a discerning glare.

continues ✐

I listen for the brass bells
to ring out and wake the town,
so I can dart for home and hide.
But they are silent.

She gives me a flirt
to steady my nerves.
But I am afraid to respond.
If only we could wait long enough,
maybe a wild gust, or
tongues of fire
might blow us together,
so we wouldn't have to suffer
this moment.

But it never comes,
so we wait patiently,
helpless,
And we hold our ground
In quiet deference
in the night,
on the church steps,
just waiting,
and never a word was said.

THE WOMAN IN THE BOWL

On nights when the moon becomes full
and white like virgin snow,
I notice a quiet woman setting a large bowl
of water on her patio
and kneeling before it—waiting patiently.

And as the moon moves across the dark sky,
enough to fully reflect in the bowl,
she cups her hands carefully beneath the image
and tries
to lift it from the water.

The moon breaks up.
And as the rippling image passes on,
I am reminded of the thousand white cranes
migrating across a distant sky

Last night, I dreamed
that I, too, had set a large bowl of water outside
in the night.
And to my surprise, a beautiful dark woman
appeared in the bowl.
I wanted to cup my hands beneath her image
and pull her gently from the bowl.

But I was afraid—and reasoned it was enough
to admire her image from afar
without the risk of losing her.
But soon, the wind blew lightly over the woman,
and a nervous ripple shook her—my heart sank.

I knew I needed to find a way to keep her
And I thought,
"If I were careful enough, oh so careful, I could pull her
From the bowl"

And I wondered if I should try.

COLOPHON

COVER & INTERIOR DESIGN/PRODUCTION
SunFlower Designs of Santa Fe
505.473.3658 • sunflowerelliott@gmail.com

TYPEFACES
Minion & Gill Sans (interior text)
University Roman (cover)

PRINTED AND BOUND IN THE UNITED STATES OF AMERICA
by CreateSpace

ORDERING INFORMATION

WRITE TO:

LIVE POETS' SOCIETY
c/o Sherry Hardage
93 Parkside Rd. SE
Rio Rancho, NM 87124

OR CALL:

1-505-670-4884

$12 Each

www.ingramcontent.com/pod-product-compliance
Lightning Source LLC
Chambersburg PA
CBHW081513040426

42447CB00013B/3215